Her Fire

Anna C. Hersh

BookLeaf Publishing

Presentation by *BookLeaf Publishing*

Web: www.bookleafpub.com

E-mail: info@bookleafpub.com

ISBN: 9789357611565

First edition 2022

I want to thank everyone who made it possible for me to publish some of my poems. I want to dedicate this book to my sister, Buggy. You believed in me before I believed in myself. Thank You!

Crumbs

You sliced into me as if I were a piece of cake.
Your mouth gorged on me,
like you had not eaten in days.
When you had your fill there was nothing left.
Only

Crumbed

      P

    i

       e

     c

      e

  s

Consent

No means no.
Does it, though?
Why does hearing my no
Make him want to still go?

Sorrow

3

A sweet face turned to stone.
Robbed of innocence,
frozen as ice.
Something inside her died that day.
Yes,
it was her fire.

Her Soul

Look into my eyes.
Do you see her?
She sees you.
The little girl trapped inside,
lonely and afraid.
Her cry echoes in the empty halls of my soul.
Her tears burn hot with shame as she is hidden
away.

Your insides decay,
full of rot and filth.
She will not escape.

You pretend not to know her,
praying she disappears.
And when it rains,
Her hope
is
washed
a
  w
    a
      y.

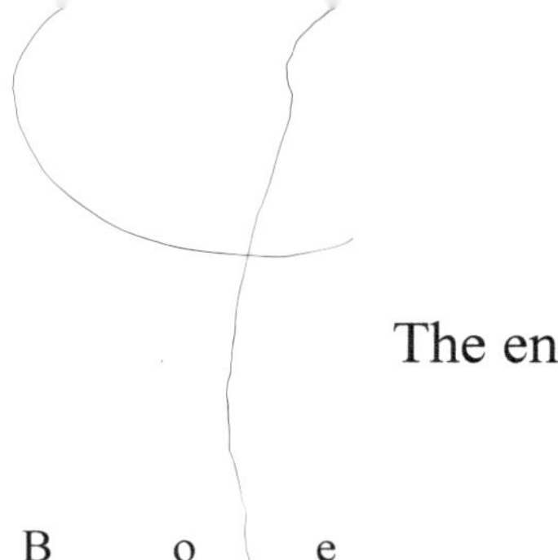

The end

B   o   e
     r   k   n

Shattered into pieces.
My body, like a corpse.
The smell, that is decay in my soul.
I am gasping for air,
But no one is there
                To hear me.

I am alone in this shallow grave,
with no hope of escape.
So, I just lay still,
I pray.

Let
this
be

the

e.n.d.

Women

Feel what they want you to feel.
Incapable, scared, and weak.

Do what they want you to do.
Sacrifice, starve, and grovel.

See yourself as they do.
Unworthy, unlovable, and broken.

Be who they want you to be.
Gentle, submissive, small
and
Silently compliant.

Always to Blame

7

Damned if you do.
Damned if you don't.

As sure as I am that the sun will rise and set.
We are always to blame.

Expectations

8

I am the help mate,
seen but not heard.
Captive in a body that is meant for one person,
And that person

is

not

me.

Together We Stand

9

Virginity is our crown,
Forged by centuries of traditions.
Worth placed on being fertile, value on our
ability to follow rules.
Keeping our heads down and we follow suit.
Is this all we are meant for?

Let us stand tall and look them in the eye.
Show the world we are strong and undeniable;
Different and all of us, incredible.
They will not shake us; they will not break us
If we stand
hand in hand.

We are far more than their traditions.

Bloom

YOU are a garden planted by others.
Some visitors have pure intentions,
While some plant weeds, choking out the
vegetation.
Only you know what your garden should grow,
What plants you desire,
And how to tend to their needs.
My dear, put on your gloves and uproot those
weeds.
Rid yourself of what no longer serves you,
And allow yourself to bloom.

For you are the gardener now.

Take Up Space

I am tired of making myself small so they can
feel tall.
There is a spark deep inside me,
Yearning to light a flame.
I am so tired of playing this game!
My worth is not based on how others view me,
It is based on how I feel about myself.

I have things to do and love to give,
This life I am choosing to live.
All voices deserve to be heard.
I have so much to say.
And on this day,
I choose to take up space.

#MeToo

Her eyes tell a story,
A cry in the depths of her hollow insides.
Deep and groaning, this sadness is hard to
disguise.
All she wants is to curl up and hide.

For I too know this kind of groan, she is not
alone.

I whisper gently as I look in her eyes:

Me too my friend,
Me too.

Grief

13

I used to hate you and push you away.
I would fight your presence every day.
But I know now what I did not know then,
You had a purpose; you were a friend.
So now I will sit with you for a while,
You have taught me it is okay, not to smile.
I will welcome your presence and allow you to
be.
And thank you for doing your part in me.

Finding Me

Broken bottle on the ground.

I look around,
I hear no sound.

The air is quiet, streets are empty.

Where do I start looking?
I am trying to find me.

The Pressure

15

Going to the gym
To restore my innocence.
Counting, weighing, and keeping a journal,
Penance for my body's iniquities.

As the pounds melted from my flesh, it was still
not enough
To get me unstuck.
Out of this pattern of reprimand and restricting.
The reflection of my nakedness left me
ashamed.
Pinching my fat, wishing it would disappear.
Then I too,
I too,
  could
    disappear.

Beauty In Our Scars

16

Your scars are proof of how strong you are.
All you have been through,
And how far you have come.
Take pride in these marks you wear,
Learn to see the beauty they bear.
My dear, you are a fighter.
Do not give up hope!
You are worthy.

Fear

17

Its roots webbed my soul,
Allowing for the venom to stick.
Necrosis sets in.
The black consumes all things light.
I might just lose this fight
For my life.

The Storm

18

Some days I do not think about it,
Others it is the only thing I can see.
Like a tornado, all-consuming and chaotic.
Rubble and debris fly through my mind crashing
into everything
In
its
way.
Piles of broken thoughts and feelings
everywhere,
I turn.

All of the sudden, stillness and silence.
Do not be fooled.
It has left its mark of desolation and destruction.
I am left empty and alone.

A Dream

My body trembles when I remember.
Not always on the outside,
But my insides are an earthquake.
As the ground shakes under me the waters rise
around me.
Stifled by the wave, I cannot speak.
I still feel his touch, his breath.
I want to run but I am frozen.
Like a dream I am watching from the outside,
hoping I will wake.
But I do not; this is not a dream.

I often have wondered, what if I did not do…
What if I did not go…
I know none of that matters though.
No matter the part I played,
It was his game.
And he is solely to blame.

Healing

It starts with a choice only you can make,
To wake up and choose today.
The journey is hard, I will not lie.
But you are more capable than you think.

Learn to trust yourself for only you know
What you need in order to grow.
Some days will be good, you will finally feel
alive!
But some days will still be hard and you may
want to hide.
Try and find joy in the small everyday things.

Allow yourself to feel.

Allow yourself to heal.

For Me

The feeling of satin on my skin,
With no pressure or expectation.
No strings or illusions, and no confusion.
Just me
Loving
Me.